STONES —AND— BONES

Powerful evidence
against evolution

STONES —AND— BONES

Powerful evidence
against evolution

Carl Wieland

Master
Books

Master Books edition
First printing: November 1996
Fourth printing: November 1999

ISBN: 0-89051-175-6

Printed in the United States of America.

Please visit our website for other great titles:
www.masterbooks.net

"This is the best brief (though extremely wide-ranging) overview of the main arguments for creation and against evolution that I know of. Easy to understand for virtually everyone, it nevertheless has sufficient depth to be suitable for the university graduate. Use it widely as a groundbreaking introduction in challenging your friends and neighbors to consider the true facts of this most vitally important of issues."

Ken Ham, B.App.Sc., Dip.Ed.
Author and renowned seminar speaker

Dr. Carl Wieland, M.B., B.S., is the chief executive officer of the Brisbane-based Creation Science Foundation Ltd., a non-profit, non-denominational evangelical ministry with affiliated organizations in Britain, New Zealand, and the USA. He has lectured and written widely on the evidence for biblical creation, and in 1978 founded the international magazine *Creation* (then *Ex Nihilo*).

The help of Dr. Len Morris (physiologist) and Dr. Andrew Snelling (geologist) in checking the text of this booklet is greatly appreciated.

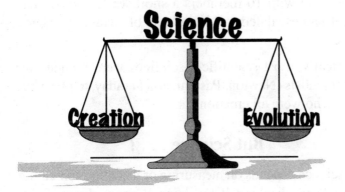

Isn't Evolution a Science and Creation Just a Religious Belief?

If this common idea were true, why would so many highly qualified scientists today accept the direct creation of a functioning world (just as it says in Genesis, the first book of the Judeo-Christian Scriptures) and reject evolution (the idea of slow self-transformation of all things from extremely simple beginnings)? In fact, the modern creation movement is a fast-growing minority.

In the United States alone, it is conservatively estimated that there are upwards of 10,000 professional scientists (the vast majority not officially linked to creation organizations) who believe in biblical creation. In 1993 in South Korea, for instance, the Korea Association of Creation Research already had a membership of over 1,000 scientists, the majority with at least a Master's or Ph.D. degree in some area of science, including 100 full-ranking university professors. The Moscow Creation Science Fellowship was formed with 10 members a short while ago. A year later, it had escalated to 120 holders of advanced science degrees.

Historically, most scientific disciplines were founded by great scientists (Newton, Pasteur, and Faraday, to name but a few) who were all creationists.

But Science . . . ?

Real science depends on measuring or watching something happen, and checking it by doing it again. Even if, for example, reptiles *did* change into birds millions of years ago, as evolutionists allege, the scientific method could never prove that as a *fact*, because it was not observed happening. If you *could* somehow turn a reptile into a bird today, even *that* wouldn't prove it happened millions of years ago. Equally, you can't insist that God should repeat the miraculous creation of many groups of birds and reptiles — all programmed to reproduce after their kind — just so you could watch it.

Both are ideas held *in faith*; each belief system (evolution or creation) offers arguments and evidences to bolster that faith. Creationists maintain that theirs is a *reasonable and logical* belief system, backed up by the weight of evidence observable in the *present*.

Do Creationists Think They Have All the Answers?

No. There are unsolved problems and unanswered questions in the creation model, but the same is true for evolution. Billions of tax dollars are spent each year trying to solve evolution-related questions; a pittance, by comparison, is spent on real creationist research.

Nevertheless, some of the seemingly difficult problems have been resolved through research by creationists in the past few years. (In the process, some previous creationist ideas and suggestions put forward in response to such problems have had to be revised or abandoned, which is normal in science.)

By evolution, we mean the non-provable (i.e., religious) belief that all things have made themselves by means of their own natural properties, with no supernatural input. Chaos has become cosmos, all by itself; particles have given rise to planets, palm trees, pelicans, and people, with no help from "outside" of the properties of matter and energy.

Theories of *how* this may have happened (i.e., the mechanisms of evolution) may come and go, but the underlying belief that it *did* somehow happen is an article of unshakable faith for many today.

Some people try to involve a "god" in such a process, but mostly, evolutionary theorists strongly reject all suggestions of any intelligent direction. Even many academic "theistic evolutionist" scientists (who claim to believe in both evolution and a god) insist that the process was entirely natural. This evolutionary "creation process" supposedly took place over billions of years in which countless creatures struggled, suffered, and died, with the strong ruthlessly wiping out the weak at many points.

Why Does It Matter?

1. Evolution justifies atheism

Everyone who insists there is no God relies upon evolution to explain nature without a designer. It is the necessary foundation for many religious world-and-life views such as atheism, agnosticism, and the associated secular humanism with its motto: "If nobody made us, nobody owns us, so there's nobody to set the rules except us." There is no logical reason to be bound by the principles set out in the Ten Commandments, for example, if other parts of the Old Testament are rejected as "cultural myths."

2. Opposite to Christianity

Running right through the entire Bible (which Christians claim is a sacred revelation from the Creator himself) is the theme that the God who consistently reveals himself therein made a *good* world (no death, struggle, violence, cruelty, or bloodshed). This entire universe has been *cursed* by God (Gen. 3, Rom. 8) as a consequence of the rebellion (sin) of the first man, Adam, against his Maker.

However, the entry of death and suffering, etc., is only a temporary intrusion, as this world will be *restored* (Acts 3:21).

CREATION

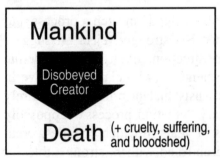

EVOLUTION

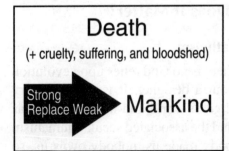

Not back to billions of years of death, cruelty, and bloodshed, but to a sinless, deathless state, because that is how it began. Jesus Christ, the Creator, made flesh (the "last Adam"), shed His innocent blood in death to redeem/ restore not only those of sinful humanity who believe, but ultimately to liberate the whole universe from this curse of death and bloodshed brought in by the first Adam.

If the evolutionary story were true, the whole point of this gospel ("good news") message would be lost, because Adam's predecessors would then have been clawing or clubbing each other to death in a world of bloodshed. It would also mean that the idea of a real, space-time fall of Adam with an associated curse on creation was a myth.

The truth of the *good news* about Jesus Christ (that people can be eternally restored to fellowship with their Creator) is utterly dependent upon the truth of the *bad news* of how our ancestor Adam rebelled, breaking that original har-mony between God and man. (1 Cor. 15:21-22 links the gospel inexorably and clearly to Adam's bringing in death: "For since by [a] man came death, by [a] man came also the resurrection of the dead. For as in Adam all die, even so in Christ shall all be made alive.") Overall, doubting Genesis has caused more and more people to doubt the rest of the Bible.

But How Do We Know That Genesis Was Written to Tell Us That Things Were Really Made in Six Days — Couldn't There Be Some Other Meaning?

If we wish to be honest, it is no longer possible to suggest that perhaps Genesis was *meant* to be something other than real, true history. According to one of the world's leading Hebrew scholars,* all the world-class university professors of Hebrew he knows of are unanimous that Genesis 1–11 was written to tell us of a real, recent creation of all things in six ordinary days and a globe-covering catastrophic flood.

That does not mean such professors necessarily *believe* it, just that the language of Genesis tells us that its writer could

---

*James Barr, Regis Professor of Hebrew at Oxford, who does not believe in the literal truth of Genesis.

not have had any other intention. It clearly means what it says, which is what has always been obvious to every ten year old.

Let's be frank — other ideas about the meaning of Genesis almost always arise — not from the Bible, but from trying to make the Bible somehow fit with *other beliefs* (such as the idea of long geological ages).

Just A Minute

If there was not death and bloodshed before Adam, you might say, what about those water-deposited rock layers around the world, containing the buried remains of billions of *dead* things?

Isn't that the sort of thing you would expect if the Bible is right about the destruction of the whole earth by water — Noah's flood? The fossils actually show signs of rapid burial, not slow and gradual processes as most people believe. For example, there are countless millions of well-preserved fossil fish, even showing scales, fins, and eye sockets. In nature, a dead fish is quickly ripped apart by scavengers and decomposes readily. Unless the fish were buried quickly, and the sediments (e.g., mud and sand) hardened fairly rapidly, such features would not be preserved.

Mother ichthyosaur (an extinct marine reptile) trapped in the process of giving birth. Such well-preserved features could not have come from mother and baby lying on the ocean floor through countless ages of slow processes. (Photo: Staatiches Museum für Naturkunde, Stuttgart)

Left: *This fish was buried so quickly it didn't even finish its lunch.*

Right: *If the layers through which such fossil tree trunks penetrate took long ages to form on top of one another, why is the top not rotted away? This sort of (polystrate) fossil is commonly found in association with coal seams.* (Photo: Steve Minkin)

Left: *Dead jellyfish literally melt away in days. The layer of sandstone near Ediacara in South Australia in which there are millions of such soft-bodied fossils, extends for thousands of square kilometers. This whole layer had to form in a day or two, with waterborne sand burying these creatures and hardening rapidly.*

But Didn't Coal Form Slowly In Swamps Over Millions Of Years?

The evidence points overwhelmingly to the *rapid* formation of coal as vast forests were uprooted and deposited, then rapidly buried. At Yallourn in Victoria (Australia), there are huge brown coal beds containing large numbers of logs of pine trees, of types which today don't grow in swamps.

Sorted, thick layers of up to 50 percent pure pollen over vast areas unmistakably show the water-borne nature of these brown coal beds. Also, many Southern Hemisphere coal deposits show no sign of anything which could represent the fossil "soil" in which the forests allegedly grew.*

Researchers at Argonne National Laboratory (USA) have taken ordinary wood fragments, mixed them with some acid-activated clay and water, heated the mixture for 28 days at only 150 degrees Celsius with no added pressure in an air-free sealed quartz tube, and obtained high-grade black coal. It doesn't need millions of years! Coal seams are known which fork (see diagrams); others connect with each other in a "Z" formation.

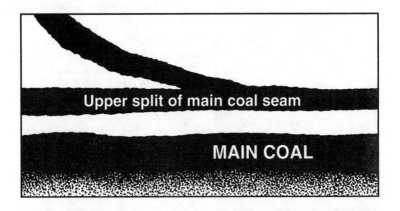

Forking in coal seam (drawn from photo [Fig. 8] in Cross, A.T., The Geology of the Pittsburgh Coal, *in pages 32-111 of the Second Conference on the Origin and Constitution of Coal, Crystal Cliffs, Nova Scotia, 1952).*

---

*The so-called "root soils" of Northern Hemisphere coals show overwhelming evidence that the stigmarian "roots" were actually floating in water, not growing in soil.

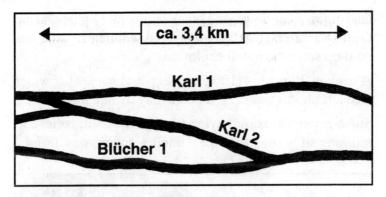

Diagram of Z-shaped coal seam connections in Germany (Raum Oberhausen-Duisburg) after Bachmann 1966 (courtesy Dr. Joachim Scheven). How could these layers represent swamps separated by millions of years?

In his 1907 report, famous Australian geologist Sir Edgeworth David described upright coalified tree trunks (like the poly-strate fossil shown on page 13) between Newcastle (Austra-lia) black coal seams that had their lower ends embedded in one coal seam, and then went right through the intervening strata to finish up in the coal seam above!

Think of trying to explain any of this by means of slow growth processes in two separate swamps separated by vast time periods. It is clear that the "slow and gradual" bias has prevented the obvious explanation for the origin of coal — rapid burial of catastrophically ripped-up vegetation by massive watery catastrophe.

Moving water, especially a lot of it, can rapidly perform an enormous amount of geological work that most people think must take millions of years. The right-hand photo on page 16 shows more than seven meters (25 feet) of layered sedimen-tary rock built up in one afternoon! This was in association with the upheaval caused by the 1980 eruption of Mount St. Helens in the state of Washington. When this mountain blew its top (and following subsequent eruptions), there were landslides, mud flows, and other sedimentary phenomena. Over 180 meters (600 feet) of layered sedimentary rock has built up since the initial explosion.

A canyon 30 meters (100 feet) deep and somewhat wider (see left photo) was carved in *one* day by *one* mud flow.*

Some experts are now saying (though they still believe in millions of years) that the Grand Canyon was formed

(Photos: Steve Austin)

catastrophically in a similar way (an enormous lake bursting its "banks"), and was *not* the result of the Colorado River's carving it out slowly over millions of years.

Do the Fossils Show Evolution?

Darwin stated, quite correctly, that if his theory was true, there should be very large numbers of "in-between types" found as fossils. If the forelimb of a reptile, for instance, has turned into the wing of a bird, why don't we find a series of fossils showing these stages — part-limb, part-wing; or part-scale, part-feather?

Darwin said that the absence of such intermediates was the "most obvious and serious objection" against his theory.

*See the video on Mount St. Helens in Recommended Materials (RM).

One hundred and twenty years later, Dr. David Raup, the head of one of the great museums in America, said that the situation concerning missing links "hasn't changed much" and that "we have even fewer examples of evolutionary transition than we had in Darwin's time."*

Dr. Colin Patterson is senior paleontologist at the British Museum (Natural History) — an evolutionist and a fossil expert. He wrote a significant book on evolution, but when someone asked him why he did not show any pictures of in-between (transitional) forms in his book, he wrote the following:**

I fully agree with your comments on the lack of direct illustration of evolutionary transitions in my book. If I knew of any, fossil or living, I would certainly have included them. You suggest that an artist should be used to visualize such transformations, but where would he get the information from? I could not, honestly, provide it, and if I were to leave it to artistic license, would that not mislead the reader?

I wrote the text of my book four years ago [in the book he does talk of his belief in some transitions — author]. *If I were to write it now, I think the book would be rather different. Gradualism is a concept I believe in, not just because of Darwin's authority, but because my understanding of genetics seems to demand it. Yet* [famous fossil expert Stephen J.] *Gould and the American Museum people are hard to*

---

*All quotations in this booklet, unless otherwise stated, are found fully referenced in *The Revised Quote Book*.

**Patterson has come under fire from fellow evolutionists for having made this and similar candid admissions, and has attempted to soften the remarks retrospectively. However, the language is clear and unmistakable.

contradict when they say there are no transitional fossils. As a paleontologist myself, I am much occupied with the philosophical problems of identifying ancestral forms in the fossil record. You say that I should at least "show a photo of the fossil from which each type of organism was derived." I will lay it on the line — there is not one such fossil for which one could make a watertight argument.

So, what do we have? Evolution expects millions of in-between forms. Some evolutionists claim there are some — maybe a handful of such in-between fossil types. Other leading evolutionist experts say there are none!

What is not often known is that the strange fossil creature *Archaeopteryx*, often used as an example of a transitional form between reptiles and birds (because it shares features found in both classes) shows none of the crucial *transitional* structures which would establish it there beyond reasonable

doubt — the feathers are fully formed, and the wings are proper wings. It has a backward-facing claw and curved feet characteristic of perching birds. It was most definitely *not*, as some would reconstruct it, a running feathered dinosaur.

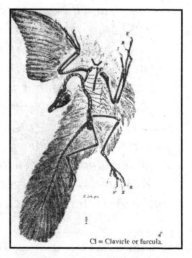

Cl = Clavicle or furcula.

Some living creatures (e.g., the platypus) are also a mosaic of features normally found in different classes. This odd little fellow, who has fur like a mammal, a beak like a duck, a tail like a beaver, venom glands like a snake, lays eggs like a reptile, yet suckles its young, is a good example of such a mosaic. It is not, however, a "halfway house" between any two of the creatures listed.

This general absence of in-between forms also applies to so-called "human evolution." This might be surprising considering that so many alleged "ancestors" are paraded. It is difficult to track all the varied and changing claims, but the past century has shown that each widely trumpeted "ancestor" claim is quietly discarded — but only when some new candidate(s) can be found to replace it. Today, much is made of the australopithecines/habilines — a broad group, of which the famous *Lucy* fossil is best known.

Dr. Charles Oxnard is one of a growing number of evolutionist anatomists who, having painstakingly examined vast numbers of measurements by computerized analysis (an objective method that does not depend on preconceived beliefs of ancestry), do not believe that these creatures are human ancestors.

He states that although initially it was thought that they were human-like or at least inter-mediate between apes and humans, the reality is that they "differ more from both humans and African apes than do these two living groups from each other. The australopithecines are unique." He indicates that the

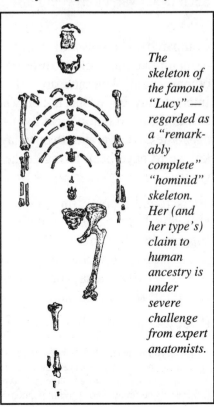

The skeleton of the famous "Lucy" — regarded as a "remarkably complete" "hominid" skeleton. Her (and her type's) claim to human ancestry is under severe challenge from expert anatomists.

non-ancestor status of these creatures is supported by an increasing number of investigators who are "independent of those representing individuals who have found the fossils."

What about so-called *Homo erectus*? Well-defined *Homo erectus* skeletal types were most probably true humans* living after the Flood and expressing bony racial variation.

Enormous variation is possible between the bones of different types of dogs, such as Chihuahuas and Great Danes. Such variation can be selected for in only a few generations. The "selection pressure" from the rapidly changing environment after the Flood, and the break up of people (after God's forced dispersion at Babel) into small, isolated populations gave ideal conditions for the rapid isolation and enhancement of (pre-existing, created) genetic differences. Such racial variation would also have included bony features.

Compared to the very wide variation in other features of the human race, the skeletal differences between *erectus* and other human skeletons are, after all, not that extreme. Interestingly, in Europe, not only *erectus*, but also Neanderthal and Cro-Magnon types (which both have larger brain capacities, on average, than today's populations) are now known to have been living at the same time as "modern" types.

Tools found recently in Indonesia in association with a *stegodon* have caused evolutionist Dr. Allan Thorne to suggest that these alleged "prehuman ancestors" had seafaring skills and technology. Quoted in the *Australian* of August 19, 1993, he says of them "They're not [i.e., shouldn't be called] *Homo erectus*, they're people."

If one uses the evolutionists' own timescales and criteria for

---

*Not everything that has been labeled *Homo erectus* — sometimes a few scraps of bone — necessarily deserves the title. Their skeletons have been found contemporaneous with those of "modern" types, and some of the *erectus* bony features can be found among living populations.

classification, and plots *all* "hominid" fossil discoveries on a chart, it will readily be seen that the idea of any evolutionary sequence is a shambles.

Do We See Evolution Happening?

In brief, no, though living things do change. Let us explain. We now know that every living thing contains a program (a set of instructions, like a blueprint or recipe) that specifies whether it will be an alligator or an avocado tree, for instance. For a human being, it specifies whether that person will have brown or blue eyes, straight or curly hair, and so forth. This INFORMATION is written on a long molecule called DNA.*

Straight hair or curly hair? The information is written on your DNA.

*DNA, as DNA, is biologically meaningless, just as a jumble of letters carries no information; it is only when the chemical "letters" that make up DNA are assembled in a specific sequence or order that it carries the INFORMATION which, when "read" by complex cellular machinery, controls the construction and operation of the organism. This sequence does *not* arise from the "internal" chemical properties of the substances which make up the DNA, in the same way that ink and paper molecules (or Scrabble letters) do not spontaneously assemble themselves into a particular message. The specific sequence of any particular DNA molecule occurs only because it is assembled under the "external" direction of the instructions carried by the DNA of the parent(s).

Evolution teaches that a comparatively simple creature, like the one-celled amoeba, has become a much more complicated one, like a horse. Even though the simplest known one-celled creatures are incredibly complex, they clearly do

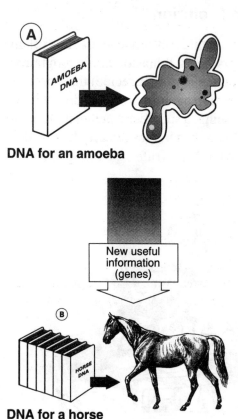

DNA for an amoeba

DNA for a horse

Real evolution requires huge increases in DNA information (symbolized here as books).

not contain as much information as, say, a horse. They don't have instructions specifying how to make eyes, ears, blood, brains, hooves, muscles. . . . So to go from A to B in the diagram would require many steps, each involving an INCREASE IN INFORMATION — information coding for new structures, new functions — new, useful complexity.

If we saw those sorts of information-increasing changes happening, even if only a few, this could reasonably be used to help support the argument that fish may, indeed, change into philosophers, given enough time. In fact, however, the many small changes we do see do not involve increasing information — they are heading in the wrong direction to be used in support of evolution, as we shall see.

Natural Selection Is Not the Same As Evolution

Living things are programmed to pass on this information to make copies of themselves, in a sense. The DNA of a man is copied and passed on via the sperm cells; that of a woman via her egg cells. In this way, the information of a mother and father is copied and passed on to the next generation. Each of us carries inside our cells two parallel long "ropes" of information — one from Mom, one from Dad* (think of it like a knotted string carrying a Morse code — in the same way, DNA has to be "read" by the complex machinery of the cell).

The reason that brothers and sisters don't all look alike is because the information combines in different ways. This reshuffling or recombination of information results in great variation in any population — humans, plants, or animals.

Consider a roomful of dogs which are all the descendants of one pair. Some will be shorter, some taller, for instance. But this normal process of variation does *NOT* involve any new

information — the information was already there in that original pair of dogs. So if a breeder *selects* those which are already shorter, then mates them, then chooses the shortest of their offspring, and so on, it is no surprise if in time a

---

*In humans, these "ropes" are as if "cut" into 23 pieces called chromosomes, but that's not important here.

"new" type of dog arises — a short breed. But no new information is involved. He has simply selected the dogs that he wants (those who are most "fit," in his view, to be allowed to pass on their genes) — and rejected the rest.

In fact, starting with the short breed only (rather than with a breed which has a mixture of tall and short types), no amount of breeding and selection will produce a tall variety, because some of the "tall" information has been lost in that population.

"Nature" can also "choose" some and reject others — in a given environment, some will be more likely to survive and pass on their information than others. Natural selection can *favor* some information above others, and can cause some of the information to be lost, but it cannot *create* any new information.

In evolutionary theory, the role of creating new information is given to mutation — random, accidental mistakes which happen as this information is copied. We know that such mistakes happen, and are inherited (because the next generation is making a copy from a defective copy). So the defect is passed on, and somewhere down the line another mistake happens, and so mutational defects tend to accumulate. This is known as the problem of *increasing mutational load* or *genetic burden*.

There are thousands of such genetic defects known in humans — known by the inherited diseases they cause. These include sickle cell anemia, cystic fibrosis, thalassemia, phenylketonuria. . . . It's no surprise to find an accidental change to a highly complex code* causing disease and dysfunction.

---

*These mistakes are not usually totally eliminated by natural selection, by the way, since most only show up as a problem if they are inherited simultaneously from both parents. Thus, one can *carry* these defects without *suffering* from them — in fact, all of us carry many such mistakes in our DNA.

Beneficial Mutations?

Evolutionists know that mutations are overwhelmingly either harmful or just meaningless genetic "noise." However, their belief system demands that there must have been "upward" mutations on occasion. There are, in fact, a tiny handful of mutations known that make it easier for an organism to survive in a given environment.

Eyeless fish in caves survive better, as they are not prone to eye disease/injury; wingless beetles do better on a windy rock in the sea because they are less likely to be blown away and drowned. But the LOSS of eyes, and the LOSS or corruption of the information necessary to manufacture wings is, however you look at it, a defect — a crippling of a previously functional piece of machinery.*

Such changes, though "beneficial" in a purely survival sense, beg the question: Where do we see any example of real, upward increases in information, new coding for new functions, new machine programs, new useful structures?

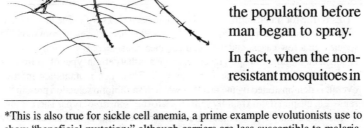

It's no use turning to insecticide resistance in insects — in almost every case** the information for resistance was there in a few individuals in the population before man began to spray.

In fact, when the non-resistant mosquitoes in

---

*This is also true for sickle cell anemia, a prime example evolutionists use to show "beneficial mutation;" although carriers are less susceptible to malaria, they have inherited a damaged gene which is no longer able to make anything other than a crippled form of hemoglobin. If inherited from *both* parents, it is a lethal disease.

**See Francisco Ayala's article "The Mechanisms of Evolution," *Scientific American*, vol. 239, no. 3, September 1978, p. 48-61.

a population are killed by DDT, for instance, and the population breeds up again from the survivors, some of the information carried by those in the (now-dead) majority is not present in the surviving minority, and so is lost forever to that population.*

When we look at the inherited changes actually happening in living things, we see information either staying the same (but recombining in different ways), or being corrupted or lost (mutation, extinction), but never do we see anything which could qualify as a real, informationally "uphill" evolutionary change.

Think About It

Isn't that exactly what you'd expect? Information theory and common sense unite to tell us that when information is transmitted (and that's what reproduction is), it either stays the same or gets less. And meaningless "noise" gets added.** Whether in living or non-living things, real information is never seen to arise or increase by itself.

Therefore, when you consider the world's biota — all its living organisms — as a whole, the total amount of information is decreasing with time, as it is being copied over and over. If one looks back in time, then, this information must increase, if anything, as one goes backwards. Since no one

---

*This is true for much antibiotic resistance in bacteria as well. The information coding for resistance may be transferred from other bacteria; even from separate species. In a few cases, mutation can enhance resistance. For example, a less efficient membrane-transport mechanism means that certain types of antibiotics are not absorbed into the bacterium as well. That such mutants are inferior overall is demonstrated by the fact that when the antibiotic selection pressure is removed, the population rapidly shifts back to the "sensitive" type. There is also at least one example of a similar situation for insecticide resistance caused by mutation.

** Examples are, copying from one audio tape to another repeatedly, or copying generation after generation of a computer program on floppy disk. At best, the information stays the same. Eventually, the tendency for it to degrade will catch up. It can be shown mathematically that this is just one more consequence of the Second Law of Thermodynamics.

suggests that one can take this process back forever (there were no finitely complex organisms living an infinite time ago), this points back to a time when this complex information had to have a beginning.

Matter left to itself (as far as real, observational science goes) does not give rise to such information, so the only alternative is that at some point a creative mind outside the system imposed intelligence on to matter (as you do when you write a sentence) and programmed all the original kinds of plants and animals. This programming of the ancestors of today's organisms must have been achieved miraculously or supernaturally, since *natural law does not create information.*

This is quite consistent with the Genesis statement that God created organisms to reproduce "after their kind." For example, a hypothetical "dog kind" created with a large amount of built-in variation (and no original defects) could vary, simply by recombinations of that original information, to give rise to wolf, coyote, dingo, and all other varieties of dogs.

Natural selection can "cull and sort" this information (but not create any more), as we saw in our mosquito example.

The differences between the resulting offspring, without any new information being added (and, therefore, no evolution), can be large enough to warrant their being called different species.

The way in which a mongrel dog population can be thinned out by artificial selection into sub-types (domestic breeds) helps us to understand this. Each sub-type carries only a fraction of the original "pool" of information. That's why, starting only with Chihuahuas, you will never be able to breed anything like a Great Dane — the necessary information is simply not there in the population any longer.

In the same way, the original "elephant kind" may have been "split" (by natural selection acting on its created information) into the African elephant, Indian elephant, the mammoth, and the mastodon (the last two now extinct).

It should be obvious, though, that this sort of change is only *within the limits* of the original information in that kind; this sort of variation/speciation does not offer any way to eventually turn an amoeba into an avocado tree, since it is not informationally "uphill" — nothing is added. Such "thinning" of the gene pool may be *called* "evolution" by some, but it does not resemble the sort of (information-adding)

change that is generally meant when the term evolution is used.*

What About the Similarities in Living Things?

One would expect a similar design for a similar structure or purpose from the hand of the same designer. The same is true of the molecular similarities — a chimpanzee is more like us than say, a bullfrog is, so one would expect this to be reflected in its internal make-up as well, such as the structure of its proteins.**

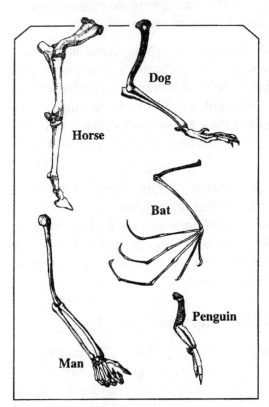

Similarities, like those shown here in the diagram of forelimb bone patterns (this is called "homology") can be explained in two ways — they all had the same ancestor OR the same designer. So their existence can hardly be called proof for *either* explanation.

But evolutionists, in fact, have

---

*For admission by a leading evolutionist that new species can form with no novel genetic information, see Lewontin, R., *The Genetic Basis of Evolutionary Change* (Columbia University Press) 1974, p. 186.

**This general principle usually holds true, though there are many exceptions for *individual* proteins that are difficult for evolutionists to explain.

some big problems here, for there are many creatures in which "homologous" structures arise from completely different parts of the embryo; from non-homologous genes; and from different embryonic segments. These are major stumbling blocks.*

Notice also that the *hind* limbs of all the creatures whose forelimb bones are shown, also have the same basic bone pattern. To be consistent, this similarity should now be interpreted to mean that they all evolved from creatures that had only one pair of limbs, which were the common ancestral structures to both forelimbs and hindlimbs.

Of course, most evolutionists would agree that this is nonsense, and would probably argue that this same pattern has evolved in both forelimbs and hindlimbs because it probably has some unknown bio-engineering advantages. But is that not then a good reason for it to be the "designer's choice" for the limbs in many different types of creatures?

Molecular biologist Michael Denton (not a creationist, incidentally) has shown that the biochemical comparisons between the proteins of different species, far from supporting evolution as is universally believed, make a strong case for the existence of discrete types (or kinds) and offer *no evidence for common ancestry*.

Evolutionary Leftovers?

Hardly anyone uses the "leftover organs'" argument any more — probably because there has been too much embarrassment in the past. Early in the twentieth century, evolutionists confidently stated that we had more than 80 organs which were useless, leftover ("vestigial") relics of our evolutionary past. One by one, functions were discovered

---

*See Sir Gavin de Beer's article in the *Oxford Biology Reader*, 1971, "Homology: An Unsolved Problem."

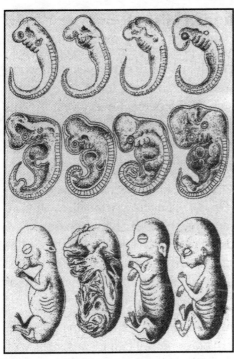

Just as office buildings, homes, and factories look similar when foundations are poured, the embryos of many different creatures are similar at first, but are each programmed to be different.

Pig   Bull   Rabbit   Man

for these, until there were hardly any left.

Even the humble appendix now appears to have a role in fighting infection, at least in early life.*

The belief that the human embryo goes through its alleged past animal stages, with gills, etc., was thoroughly discredited a long time ago, but dies hard.**

---

*See Glover, J.W., "The Human Vermiform Appendix — A General Surgeon's Reflections," *Ex Nihilo Technical Journal*, vol. 3, 1988, p. 31-38.

** At one Australian university, the vast majority of fifth-year medical students were found to believe that gills form in the human embryo, even though their third-year embryology textbook says that they do not. (See *Creation* magazine, vol 14., no. 3, 1992, p. 48.

Human History

In modern times, human populations are seen to be increasing consistently at more than 1 percent per year. Allowing for disease, famine, wars, and so forth, let us take a much more conservative figure of 0.5 percent every year. At this rate, it would take only around 4,000 to 5,000 years, starting with eight people at Mount Ararat, to reach today's population.

It is well-documented that racist attitudes skyrocketed after Darwin published his *Origin of Species*. After all, evolutionists believed that the races had been evolving separately for hundreds of thousands of years, so it was logical that this "progress" was happening at different rates; therefore, some races were not as far removed from their animal ancestors as others.

Modern genetics shows, however, that all human peoples (or races) are extremely close biologically, consistent with all the racial characteristics having been present in one small ancestral population, which was then "split" into subgroups at Babel.*

Many are surprised to learn, for instance, that there is only ONE main coloring pigment in humanity. What shade of black, white, or brown you are depends on how much you have of this substance called *melanin*. Since all of the

---

*For details, see "The Origin of Races" in *The Answers Book* (RM).

created characteristics in the human population were present in Noah's family (and before that in Adam and Eve), we can deduce that they were most probably mid-brown individuals, with dark hair and brown eyes.

Incidentally, the alleged "problem" about Cain's wife having to be a close relative (Genesis 5:4 indicates that Adam and Eve had daughters, too), far from being a challenge to the truth of Genesis, actually strengthens it! Since mutation-caused defects, occurring after a fault-free beginning, take time to accumulate over generations, Adam's offspring need not have feared deformities in the children of close marriages for many centuries. Even Abraham could marry his half-sister safely, and the moral law against incest was, therefore, not given until Moses' time, hundreds of years later.

If human races have split from the descendants of those who survived such a colossal catastrophe as Noah's flood, is it not logical to expect widespread memories of such an awesome event in stories and legends? In fact, whether Australian Aborigines, Arctic Eskimos, or American Indians, virtually every tribe and nation on earth has such a flood story.

Though distorted by time and retelling, the parallels with Genesis are often remarkable, frequently including the sending out of the birds and the after-Flood sacrifice, for example. Even, sometimes, the rainbow is present and the correct number of people saved — eight.

EIGHT

VESSEL

MOUTH

The ancient Chinese pictogram for "boat" (shown) is a combination of the symbols for a vessel, and for eight mouths (people).

Many traditions also have accounts similar to the dispersion of tongues at Babel, but not stories of Moses' Red Sea crossing, for example, because this happened *after* people separated at Babel. (These Flood/Babel stories did not come from Christian missionaries.)

A tablet exists of a Mesopotamian Flood story with many similarities to Genesis. Those not disposed to accepting the Bible as God's Word insist it shows that the Hebrews borrowed the Flood story from surrounding cultures. However, this evidence is exactly what one would expect if the Genesis account of Noah is true — memories of the Flood would be less corrupted in cultures closer (geographically and in time) to the Middle East, than those more removed, such as the Flood legends of Amerindians and Aboriginal Australians.

Doesn't Radiometric Dating "Prove" an Old Earth?

There are, in fact, many dating methods which give upper limits to the age of the earth and universe far less than evolution requires. Some point to an age of a few thousand years at most. Naturally, evolutionists will automatically, even unconsciously, prefer methods (e.g., most radiometric methods) which allow enough time to make their transformist belief seem possible.

Contrary to popular belief, carbon-dating has nothing to do with millions of years (even with the best analytical equipment today, its upper limit is around 100,000 theoretical

A waterwheel at Cape Leeuwin, Western Australia, entombed in solid rock in less than 65 years. (From an article in *Creation* magazine, vol. 16, no. 2, Marcy–May 1994, p 25. Photo: Bev Lunt)

years). It is a method that can date only those things which still contain organic carbon (unlike most fossil bones, for example). When the method and all its assumptions are understood and checked against real-world data, it is actually a powerful argument for a young world (see *The Answers Book*).

Another popular belief is that radiometric methods generally agree with each other. Perhaps this belief has arisen because of an unconscious "selection" process. As evolutionist Professor Richard Mauger says, "In general, dates in the 'nearest ballpark' are assumed to be correct and are published, but those in disagreement with other data are seldom published nor are discrepancies fully explained."

Carbon-dating of wood *under* lava that was erupted from Rangitoto (an island volcano near Auckland, New Zealand) indicates that the eruption was around 200 years ago (the name is said to mean "red sky," suggesting that the Maoris, who have been there for 1,000 years at the most, witnessed this event). Yet, potassium-argon dating of the lava has given ages of up to half a million years! (*Creation* magazine, vol. 13, no. 1, 1991, p. 15). Incidentally, this method is used on occasion to "date" fossils by their associated lava flows.

What About Dinosaurs?

You might have wondered why it is that so many cultures have legends of dragons — great, reptilian beasts, featuring horns, scales, armor plating (and some of these dragons flew) — which are remarkably similar to the fossil-based reconstructions of dinosaurs and other extinct reptiles; yet we are told that no man has ever seen a dinosaur *or* a dragon. The Bible actually mentions dragons (the Hebrew word is *tnn (tannin)* — the word "dinosaur" was not invented until the nineteenth century).

If we take biblical history at face value, then the notion of men and dinosaurs having lived together in the past is not so difficult. Many creatures have become extinct — it is happening even today. Extinction is not evolution, and there is no fossil evidence of dinosaurs having evolved from non-dinosaurs.*

Biology By Chance?

Consider the incredible improbabilities involved in getting the whole evolutionary scenario started in the first place. People talk as if it were somehow an observed FACT — but the fact is that no one really has any sort of scientific explanation for *how* the complicated, information-bearing molecules required for even the simplest conceivable "first life" could have arisen without outside intelligence. And there are good scientific reasons for believing this to be *impossible*.

It's often overlooked that the properties of a cell which make it alive cannot be explained by just referring to the chemical

*There is even a probable description of a dinosaur in the Bible — behemoth in Job 40.

properties of its building blocks, in the same way the total properties of a car cannot be explained by the properties of rubber, metal, plastic, and so forth. The idea or concept "car" had to be imposed onto the raw matter from the "outside," as it were. It takes matter/energy plus INFORMATION, which is a non-material property that is carried on matter, but does not reside *in* matter.*

If I can just create life here, it will prove that no intelligence was necessary in the beginning.

If all it took were the right ingredients, why don't we see a fish in a sardine can occasionally spring back to life? Perhaps it would happen if energy were added? Of course not! It takes much more than energy plus the right ingredients; it requires order, organization — INFORMATION. Living things get their information from their parent organisms, but we *NEVER* see information arising from raw, unprogrammed matter.

It is hard to see logically how evolutionary selection mecha-

---

*The total properties of this page, which include the ideas it conveys, cannot be reduced to the properties of ink and paper — but to ink plus paper plus INFORMATION — the exact sequence in which the letters have been arranged on the page. I can transfer the information "the cat sat" from mind to computer disk to pen and ink; though the information is being transferred from one type of matter to another, the matter itself is not what is being transferred.

nisms are of any use to the theory until you have self-replicating, programmed machinery, such as characterizes all life, already in existence. Yet all known life depends on information-bearing polymers. These are long-chained molecules whose function depends on the sequence in which the sub-units are assembled — just as the function of a computer program depends on the sequence in which the commands have been programmed.

That means that evolutionists have to believe in INFOR-MATION having arisen by PURE CHANCE. Non-creationist Sir Fred Hoyle says in his book *Evolution from Space* that the odds against even *ONE* such polymer arising by chance from a random "soup" are about the same as filling the solar system shoulder to shoulder with blind men all randomly shuffling Rubik's cubes and having them all, by pure chance, solve the puzzle at the same time!

Why Then Do So Many People Believe Strongly In Evolution?

There are, of course, many reasons: social/cultural pressures, not having a chance to consider alternatives, academic upbringing. But the Bible indicates that another, deeper reason should also be considered. It refers to the fact that humanity, since the rebellion of its first representative Adam, has an innate tendency to oppose the Creator's rule over their lives.

In Romans 1:18-22, we read the following:

> *For the wrath of God is revealed from heaven against all ungodliness and unrighteousness of men, who hold the truth in unrighteousness; because that which may be known of God is manifest in them; for God hath showed it unto them. For the invisible things of him from the creation of the world are clearly seen, being*

understood by the things that are made, even his eternal power and Godhead; so that they are without excuse: because that, when they knew God, they glorified Him not as God, neither were thankful; but became vain in their imaginations, and their foolish heart was darkened. Professing themselves to be wise, they became fools.

The Choice

You can continue to believe in evolution by faith, or choose to believe in creation by faith. Belief in creation is not only scientifically reasonable, but it makes much more common sense. Stand back and take a look at this incredibly complex, interacting world, not to mention the astonishing human

(Illustration © Films for Christ)

brain, and then think of the belief that all of this came from *nothing,* ultimately *by chance*! Surely, such a belief involves blind faith, rather than the reasonable faith of the creationist.

If it all came about on purpose, due to the deliberate actions of a great intelligence acting, then the only way we could know about the purpose of the universe is if it has been revealed to us, which it has. The Bible is unique, and claims over 3,000 times to be the reliable communication of the Creator himself, telling us about that purpose.

Are you concerned or puzzled about death and suffering in a world made by God? Because Genesis is true, we can know why such things exist and also know that they are not a permanent part of creation for all time.*

The ugly aspects of nature are because (as a result of Adam's disobedience) it is a ruined, cursed creation, which, nevertheless, still shows remnants of its original beauty and total goodness.

The people who have published this booklet are not interested in getting you to join a particular group or church denomination. They want you to face up to the evidence that the world was created *by* Jesus Christ and *for* His purposes (Col. 1:16). They want you to be reconciled to your Creator, the sinless God, and to the Son who was made flesh, suffered, and died, then rose from the dead.

He bore the penalty for your sins against a Holy God, the Father whose laws we all have broken, so that you might repent and cast yourself on His infinite mercy and grace on the basis of Christ's blood sacrifice on your behalf. Then you will not only have life more abundantly now, but *eternal* life with Him, rather than condemnation for eternity (John 3:18).

Why not read the Bible right now? A good way to begin is as follows: Read the first 11 chapters of Genesis to understand the true history of the world. Then Exodus 20:1-17, the Law of God, followed by the Gospel of John. You are encouraged to discuss these matters with the leadership of a reputable, Bible-believing Christian church in your neighborhood.

If you are a Christian already, we want to urge you to understand the realities behind this crucial spiritual battle of

---

*A suggestion about the question of why God allowed sin to enter creation: For there to be the possibility of true love between man and God, mankind had to be created with a free will capable of rejecting that love (i.e., capable of sin).

creation/evolution. We see the lethal fruits of the increasing acceptance of evolution all around us, as society more and more accepts the philosophy that "no one made us, so we can do as we please."

The logical foundations of Christianity are under attack as never before, yet never before have there been so many good, solid answers available for Christians to defend their faith and to use to see others won to our Lord and Saviour, Jesus Christ.

Modern Creation Trilogy

Volume I - Scripture and Creation
Volume II - Science and Creation
Volume III - Society and Creation

Dr. Henry M. Morris
and Dr. John D. Morris

The definitive work on the study of origins, from a creationist perspective, *The Modern Creation Trilogy* examines the evidences for both evolution and special creation. Authored by the prolific father-son research team of Henry and John Morris, this three-volume gift set is a "must-have" for those who believe the Bible is God's plain-spoken Word.

Volume I looks at what the Bible says about origins — man, animal, planet, and universe. Volume II studies the scientific evidences for evolution and creation, contending that the evidence favors creation, since none of us were there in the beginning. Volume III sheds light on the fruits of each worldview — which stance produces better results for all creation? Interest level: Adult.. CD Rom included.

ISBN: 0-89051-216-7
Gift-boxed set of three • Paperback • 5-1/4 x 8-1/2 • $44.95

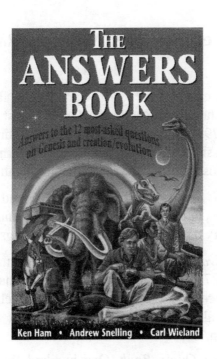

The Answers Book

Ken Ham • Andrew Snelling • Carl Wieland

With answers to the 12 most-asked questions on Genesis and creation/evolution, this book offers in-depth analysis of such topics as: the origin of races, continental drift, dinosaurs, the Gap Theory, and carbon dating. Loaded with helpful illustrations, this book has proven to be tremendously popular as a "cat-call" book for those who witness and build up the faith of believers.

ISBN: 0-89051-161-6
Paperback • 5-1/4 x 8-1/2 • $10.95

Recommended Materials (RM)

Books

Dry Bones and Other Fossils, Gary Parker, illustrated by Jonathan Chong and Ron Hight (Green Forest, AR: Master Books, 1979). An entertaining look at the Parker family's hunt for fossils, explaining how fossils are formed. Emphasizes that fossils are strong evidence for Noah's Flood.

The Genesis Record, Henry M. Morris (Grand Rapids, MI: Baker Book House, 1979). A scientific and devotional commentary on the whole book of beginnings.

The Lie: Evolution, Ken Ham (Green Forest, AR: Master Books, 1987). Excellent and important layman's book on the *relevance* aspects of Creation. A clear teaching book on how to deal with the issue, without a lot of technical information.

The Revised Quote Book. One hundred thirty carefully checked quotations from evolutionists themselves, in easy-to-find subject groups. Devastating admissions laying bare the myth of evolution. Published by Creation Science Foundation, Australia; distributed in the United States by Master Books.

What is Creation Science? Henry M. Morris and Gary Parker (Green Forest, AR: Master Books, 1982). A semi-technical review of the evidence from physical and biological sciences supporting creation, with no religious references.

The Young Earth, John D. Morris (Green Forest, AR: Master Books, 1994). A study, from a trained geologist, of the geologic evidence to support a young earth theory. Plenty of detailed information presented in an easy-to-read style.

Videos

Mount St. Helens: Explosive Evidence for Catastrophe in Earth's History. Graphic footage showing canyons, rock layers, and much more formed in mere days. Produced by the Institute for Creation Research; available from Master Books.

What Really Happened to the Dinosaurs? Brilliant illustrated talk for nearly all ages by Ken Ham. Part of "Answers in Genesis," a 12-video set, available from Master Books.

For more information on the complete Master Books line, a catalog, and previews of upcoming projects, please write to:

Master Books
P.O. Box 727
Green Forest, AR 72638